WIDE OPEN FEAR

WRITER CHAPS

SHORT BOOKS FULL OF OUTSTANDING ADVICE FROM AUSTRALIA'S TOP SPECULATIVE FICTION WRITERS

Season One

You Are Not Your Writing and Other Sage Advice, Angela Slatter

From Baby Brain To Writer Brain: Writing Through A World of Parenting Distractions, Tansy Rayner Roberts

Eyes on the Stars: Writing Science Fiction & Fantasy, Sean Williams

The Martial Art of Writing and Other Essays, Alan Baxter

Capturing Ghosts on the Page, Kaaron Warren

Headstrong Girl: How To Live A Writer's Life, Kim Wilkins

Season Two

What To Do When You Don't Have A Book Coming Out & Even More Sage Advice, Angela Slatter

Wide Open Fear, Lisa L. Hannett

WIDE OPEN FEAR

Collected Southern Dark Columns

LISA L. HANNETT

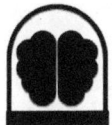

Brain Jar Press
PO Box 6687
Upper Mt Gravatt, QLD, 4122
Australia
www.BrainJarPress.com

Copyright © 2022 by Lisa L. Hannett

The moral right of Lisa L. Hannett to be identified as the author of this work has been asserted.

All rights reserved. No part of this book may be reproduced in any form or by any electronic or mechanical means, including information storage and retrieval systems, without written permission from the author, except for the use of brief quotations in a book review.

Cover design by Peter Ball
Cover Image: *Marreee Australian Outback isolated house,* Zorro Stock Images /Shutterstock; *Silence Before The Storm*, Cekal/Shutterstock.

ISBN: 978-1-922479-33-4 (Ebook) | 978-1-922479-34-1 (Chapbook)

Contents

On Behalf of Neglected Night Creatures	1
A Dreadful Fear of Clichés	6
The 'I' In Horror	12
After Fight Club	20
Wide Open Fear	30
About the Author	39

On Behalf of Neglected Night Creatures

It's not that I hate vampires and zombies.

Like many fans of dark fiction, I was once seduced by Bram Stoker's *Dracula* and Le Fanu's *Carmilla* and Anne Rice's *Interview with the Vampire*. I watched all of *Buffy* and some of *Angel*. The first season of *True Blood* was intriguing, as was its premise, though the show quickly wore thin. I still consider Norman Partridge's 'Apotropaics' (Subterranean Press, 2008) one of the most refreshing uses of vampire lore in short fiction. Jason Nahrung's *Blood and Dust*(2012), what will no doubt prove to be a rollicking vampire yarn set in the Queensland outback, is a novel I'm really looking forward to reading. And James Bradley has written a brilliant essay, 'Bloody Beauties: The Rise and Rise of Vampire Lit' (*The Australian Literary Review*), which has done an excellent job explaining the resilience of vampire fiction over the years.

Also, I adore all of Kelly Link's zombie stories and gobble new ones up as soon as they're published. Maureen McHugh's 'The Naturalist' (*After the Apocalypse*) employs a familiar 'plague/virus' trope, but does something so wonderfully horrible with it that it was a joy to read. In a similar vein, Felicity Dowker's 'Bread and Circuses' (the titular story of her 2012 collection) has sparked many a conversation about the new directions zombie tales can take. And the first season of *The Walking Dead* is on my shelf *as we speak*, just waiting to be watched.

But.

Even so.

I'm here with a plea on behalf of *other* night creatures, those poor dark ones who've been sadly neglected while narratives about vampires and zombies have reached critical mass:

Why not write more about us?

If you're keen to write tales of bloodsuckers, there are other options. The 'homunculus' is commonly treated as a representation of a human, like a doppelganger, a mannequin, or Frankenstein's monster, but reading Agrippa's description of this little thing shows that it might well be considered an alternate blood-fiend. Agrippa explains that a homunculus is a tiny, perfectly formed human spawned in a glass jar (which is subsequently buried in a dunghill), who 'is fed each day on the arcanum of human blood for a span of 40 weeks...' Sure, it's easy to see the metaphor for conception and gestation inherent in this description, much as 17th century scholars did when describing the tiny 'animalcules' — the miniature people — inhabiting individual sperm. Nevertheless, taken literally, the homunculus could be a chilling addition to horror tales. Just think jars and blood and tiny trapped people and let your imaginations run wild from there....

Then there are the lamiae (sing. Lamia). Ancient Greek mythology refers to lamiae as monstrous, demonic, child-eaters — which is horrific enough in itself. But delving into the motivations behind this devouring of children could provide great fodder for modern horror stories. According to Topsell's *The Historie of Foure-Footed Beastes* (1607), a different version of the lamia is 'a scaly, four-legged creature, with hoofs behind and paws in front, with a woman's face, a hermaphrodite with a man's organ and woman's breasts.' In addition, some sources say lamiae are shapeshifters who also have the power of invisibility. A blood-sucking, hermaphroditic chimera who can appear and disappear at will, you say? Yes, please!

Meanwhile, John Keats' poem 'Lamia' (1819) seems to have influenced the Western collective unconscious by giving form to the lamiae we're most familiar with in popular culture today. Keats' lamia is a beautiful woman who transforms into a vampish snake creature, often human above and serpent below:

> She was a gordian shape of dazzling hue,
> Vermilion-spotted, golden, green, and blue;
> Striped like a zebra, freckled like a pard,
> Eyed like a peacock, and all crimson barr'd ...
> So rainbow-sided, touch'd with miseries,
> She seem'd, at once, some penanced lady elf,
> Some demon's mistress, or the demon's self...

In *Love and Romanpunk*, Tansy Rayner Roberts offers two stories that feature lamiae: 'Lamia Victoriana' and 'Julia Agrippina's Secret Family Bestiary' (which includes, among others, the basilisk, centaur, harpy, and manticore along with vampires and werewolves) — both of which are welcome additions to lamia lore.

Another well-known, but lately underrepresented, denizen of the dark is the sin-eater, that human vehicle for the sins of the dead. Essentially, the deceased's sins — or, if you prefer your horror *sans* Christian connotation, we can call them *guilts* or *sorrows* — were transferred through the ritual of eating food that had been in contact with the 'sinner's' corpse. M. John Harrison explored this notion in his story 'Strange Great Sins', as did Leigh Blackmore in his piece 'Soul Food'. The novel *Sineater* by Elizabeth Massie, which won the 1992 Bram Stoker Award, explores sin-eating in an Appalachian context. What makes this concept perpetually intriguing is the idea of a living person being a scapegoat for the dead — how did they come to be in this position? What do they do with the sins they've ingested? And how do they ever shuck this role?

Some other, more esoteric, characters I'd love to see in fiction include the haruspex, one who uses entrails for the purpose of divination. Traditionally, animal parts were used for haruspicy — but one of the joys in writing is creative reinvention. Surely I can't be the only one whose mind leaps to horror-crime scenarios, where the intestines being read aren't only animal.... Or how about stories featuring capnomancers, those who use smoke the way haruspices use guts? The practice of libanomancy deals more specifically with burning incense to interpret smoke patterns, but a capnomancer is more flexible; (s)he inhales the smoke rising from many different burning things, including human sacrifices.... These magic-workers want to breathe the fire's breath — its ghost, its death. And as great swathes of Australia are currently burning with bushfires, capnomancy seems particularly relevant; pair them with pyromancers, and who knows what havoc they could wreak?

There are also hags and harpies who, like the early lamiae, were known to suck vitality from children. One Scottish night-prowler, carrying a wizened baby and wearing her trademark green cloak, would enter people's houses in search of infants' blood. And in the hills of Leicester, folklore tells us, there is a hag's cave in which the walls are adorned with the skins of small children.... Skins which could, perhaps, be used in stitching together Jenny Hanivers? These shrivelled cockatrices and forged mermaids, which feature in many carnival sideshows, would be almost as disturbing this way as they are in J.J. Irwin's creepy story 'Haniver' (*Shimmer* 13). And still there are yowies, like the one in Thoraiya Dyer's 'Yowie' (*Sprawl*), and there are rhapsodomancers — sorcerers who read bits of poetry out at random for oracular purposes — and there are manticores and chimaeras and duppies and corpse-stealing kashas and zashiki-warishis and and and … and too many others to mention in a short column.

It is possibly easier to depict timeworn creatures than it is to write about, say, basilisks or wendigos. The mythos surrounding vampires and zombies has pervaded popular culture to such an extent that it's possible to take shortcuts when writing. A throwaway mention of garlic, lack of reflection, a global plague or an inexplicable hunger for braaiinnnssss is enough to let readers instantly know who these monsters are and how they function. But despite their enduring appeal, it might just be time to give vampires and zombies a break. Let them recede into the shadows for a while — and bring some of the more neglected night creatures into the spotlight.

A Dreadful Fear of Clichés

I have a confession. There are a few (well, *many*) horror tropes that I just cannot stomach at all. Not because they're cliché — although, of course, they *are* — but because there's something about them that's actually, fundamentally, terrifying.

The first involves revenants, namely the twitchy-jittery and/or fast-moving variety. True, this is one of the most hackneyed techniques used in horror movies nowadays — but still. Logically I can figure out how the twitchy-fast effect is achieved. Most likely, it's a combination of camerawork and post-production trickery. The film is sped up; actors' movements are edited so they seem to randomly jump across the screen; filters or dark obscuring layers are added so the creatures are blurred, and hard to get a fix on. I know this, I can work this out, *logically*.

But, alas, fear isn't necessarily controlled by logic.

Rationalising how Samara flickers out of the TV in *The Ring* — or how Kayako's ghost jitter-crawls down the stairs in *The Grudge* — or how the spooky little girl in the video game *F.E.A.R.* shudders down hallways — or how spectral doctors flash across video screens in the (otherwise lame) *House on Haunted Hill* — doesn't stop me from whimpering like a puppy when I see them. The same applies when zombies or 'infected' people scuttle and jerk in films like *28 Days Later* or *Zombieland*, or when they race at incredible speeds, as it seems will happen in *World War Z*.

Whimpering.

Puppy.

These creatures' super-quick movements play on the innate fear of being chased; of falling prey to a hunter that is stronger and faster than we are. This feeling of dread intensifies when the fast-movers appear in packs. Our survival instincts scream that we're not only too slow to outrun them — we're also doomed because we're outnumbered. And yet it's not just the sense of being pursued that makes these 'monsters' intensely scary. Seeing a film in which people are chased by wild dogs or wolves or demonic piranhas is nowhere near as frightening as watching zombies barrel after them at full tilt — even though the outcome of getting caught (being mutilated, ravaged, devoured, killed) is more or less the same in each case. The problem, then, isn't just that the ghosts and zombies are fast or spasmodic. It's the fact that they are — or were — people.

People shouldn't be able to move like that.

Granted, death and curses and global plagues have altered these people in horrifying ways. That is, you wouldn't expect to see them acting within *logical* social conventions: picking the grommets up from afterlife care; heading down to the 7-11 for a brain slushie; bemoaning their depressing unlives on 'Being Human'. The frightening ones are deeply chilling because they are uncanny. They are *almost* right and still oddly wrong. They are familiar — we can easily recognise their humanoid forms, possibly even their previous identities — but simultaneously unfamiliar. They look like people, so our subconscious tells us they should behave as such. But, obviously, they don't. They are freakishly unpredictable. They jerk. They move in all the wrong directions. They are essentially mindless and yet single-minded in their ambitions. We can guess what they want — revenge, blood, prey — but we cannot reason with them. With these creatures, the main 'reason' seems to be the primal one: kill, or be killed.

It's an unsettling thing to witness from the comfort of our living rooms, even though, logically, we know we're not in any real danger.

This uncanny portrayal of almost-humans partially explains why a second overused horror trope — the ceiling-crawler — also inspires puppy-dog whimpering. Gravity and perception have conspired to convince us that people usually walk (or roll in wheelchairs or use crutches) on the ground, not on ceilings. And when they do, their arms and legs generally swing in recognisable, rhythmic motions. Limbs aren't meant to bend backwards at the elbow, or suction onto walls, or jut out at impossible angles. Again, on one level, the contorted configurations the body adopts when it scuttles across a ceiling are disturbing because they defy logic. More to the point, they just don't look right. Add to this uncanniness the fact that in many films — such as *The Exorcist, The Exorcist III, Constantine, Legion, Messengers* — the 'crawlers' aren't robust and muscular, but instead the sorts of people we tend to feel protective of in 'real life' (children, young girls, old ladies) and ceiling-crawling becomes even more unsettling. And if this wasn't enough to put a churn in the belly, there's the additional fact that the crawling is often caused by demonic possession or some other sort of soul-displacement. So, on top of the uncanniness, what is scary here is the loss of humanity and agency. These are bodies that look but don't act like people. They are themselves, but simultaneously under supernatural control — and, as such, beyond ours.

I should point out that not *all* ceiling-crawling achieves this effect. It is theoretically shocking to have a baby crawling across a ceiling, with a head that spins around like Regan's in *The Exorcist*; however, when this happens in *Trainspotting*, the effect is undermined by the fact that the 'baby' is so terribly fake. Its movements are laughably unnatural and mechanical; its face is cartoonish, a badly constructed wax doll. And though dolls can certainly be both uncanny and terrifying — this one just isn't. We understand the horror of the situation — the baby has died of neglect, after all — but the not-so-special effects are enough to throw viewers out of the moment, and so diminish the sense of unease.

Similarly, it is startling to see sharp-toothed aliens in the *Alien* films unfurl themselves from ship-walls and ceilings; heart-pounding to watch them stalk and ultimately pounce on the human prey below. These creatures get the blood and adrenaline pumping. And, sure, if the music and lighting and timing are just right, they make you jump. However, watching patently non-human creatures behave like gut-driven predators is somehow less frightening than seeing *human* dead hunt the living — or, at least, these aliens are frightening in a different way. They are terrifying, but we are not exactly *repulsed* when they crawl overhead. Watching aliens act in an alien fashion is fairly logical; it makes sense that they'll do things beyond the sphere of expected human behaviour. By contrast, watching ex-people behave in an alien manner inspires feelings of revulsion. It makes us shudder rather than scream in surprise. In other words, it creeps us out.

Likewise, the third horror trope I want to mention here: humans with black inky-scribbly eyes. I've intentionally added 'scribbly' to this description to differentiate these characters from the many, many black-sclera-lensed baddies that have appeared on screens (large and small) in the past twenty-odd years. Fully-black eyes usually indicate a character's 'evilness' or his/her possession by something 'evil', as is the case in *Buffy, True Blood, Being Human, Supernatural, 30 Days of Night, Hellraiser* — or, in *Babylon 5*, they depict non-demonic possession (but possession nonetheless) when Lyta Alexander is taken over by her Vorlon side. Eyeballs without irises or pupils — whether blackened, as these are, or blanked by white cataracts — are disconcerting if only because they represent blindness and, by extension, the fear many of us would feel at being unable to see. Even so, the former are often more unnerving than the latter because they are supernatural. Sure, they are familiar — because this trope is now commonplace — but nevertheless, strange. When those black lenses slip into place, we can no longer make eye contact with the person bearing them. We can't engage with them on an intellectual or emotional level. We can't see through the 'window into their soul'. Whatever they were — whatever made them human — is masked behind this darkness. Instead of using reason and logic to communicate, we're forced to relate to them on physical, instinctive, unpredictable, primal levels. And somehow, though they are blind, they can still see us ... which is as freaky as hell.

In *Over Her Dead Body: Death, Femininity and the Aesthetic* (1992), Elisabeth Bronfen raises a point about vision and blindness — which, she observes, 'are integral to Freud's discussion of the uncanny' — that sums up what I find so frightening about scribbly-black eyes like the ones in Joe Hill's *Heart-Shaped Box*. It is the 'undecidable border phenomena' mentioned in this discussion that is particularly relevant here:

> ...whether something is animate (alive) or inanimate (dead), whether something is real or imagined, unique, original or a repetition, a copy, cannot be decided.

In other words, when we are confronted by human-shaped characters with scribbly-black eyes, it is almost impossible to determine — on first glance — if these people are alive or dead, seeing or unseeing, real or imaginary. Is this figure a ghost? *Can* they still see even though their eyes are squirming with ink? How do human eyes *move* like that? Is this thing still alive? Is this a hallucination? Is this person beyond hope of being saved? The narrative's unfolding action soon answers these questions — but it was that first, uncertain glance that forced me to put *Heart-Shaped Box* down, unable to continue reading until morning.

There are many other horror tropes that, for similar reasons, could have been included here. Demonic voices emanating from children. Whispers coming from everywhere and nowhere. Shadows flitting without any bodies nearby to cast them. Revenants appearing in unexpected places (the bed, the bathroom, etc) but doing nothing but standing there, *staring*. No doubt there are even more than these — but let's leave them in the darkness for now. There's only so much dread this poor whimpering puppy can handle at once.

The 'I' In Horror

Writers of great horror don't hold back when it comes to subject matter: nothing is off limits. Their stories go places that make readers shudder, sweat, squirm. Settings may be familiar, but somehow they are also warped. 'Natural' elements are inevitably of the 'un' or 'super' variety. Plots are designed to unnerve. In horror, the depths of the human psyche are dredged; dark secrets, dark fears, dark realities are unearthed, then strewn in black ink across paper. And when the tale is told, the last page turned, the best authors will leave us hoping never to meet anyone, in real life, as disturbed as the characters they've created. We like to pretend that such people live *out there, somewhere else* — that they'll always be anonymous strangers.

But then we read horror stories in which authors are also characters, and we are forced to drop such comfortable pretences.

There's a long history of authors writing themselves into their narratives in genre fiction. To name but a few: Philip K. Dick does it in his time-travel SF novel *VALIS* (1981) and in a tricky postmodern way PKD also makes an appearance in his short story 'Orpheus with Clay Feet' (1964). Charles Yu is the protagonist in his award-winning *How to Live Safely in a Science Fictional Universe* (2011) and Paul Auster appears in various ways (as Paul Auster) in his literary crime series *The New York Trilogy* (1987). Bringing it back to horror, all flavours of self-reflexivity, self-consciousness, and self-insertion are features of the film *Wes Craven's New Nightmare* (1994) and Tobe Hooper's novel *Midnight Movie* (2011).[1] In Stephen King's metatextual *Dark Tower* series, the author makes a pivotal appearance in the narrative that allows the main characters to get on with their quest — and King also appears in *Song of Susannah* (2004). In these cases, the concept of author-as-character might be playful, but it isn't pastiche. We don't read these texts the way we do, say, the *Scary Movie* series of films; these books aren't presented as spoofs of their given genres.

The works I'm going to focus on here —Lunar Park by Bret Easton Ellis (2005) and a few short stories by Paul Haines — feature authors as protagonists in complex and interesting ways. Their respective works are set in real places — Australia for Haines, Los Angeles, New York and New England for Ellis — and even a quick scan of Wikipedia is enough to situate the authors within these settings in 'real' life. As characters, Ellis and Haines are quintessential unreliable narrators; instead of reassuring readers, the use of their 'real' names in these 'unreal' scenarios instantly unsettles. Lines between fact and fiction are blurred: the blurb on the back of *Lunar Park*, for instance, describes the book as 'part autobiography, part fantasy' and it isn't always easy to figure out where one ends and the other begins.

In *Lunar Park*, Ellis begins by presenting a potted history of his rise to literary stardom. There's money, drugs, hedonism — it's the heyday of late 20th century capitalism in American publishing circles. Peppered with references to

Ellis's other novels and characters, the book is overtly, self-consciously meta-to-the-max right from the start. As the story progresses, gesturing at his other works becomes a kind of full-armed pointing that is impossible to miss. Take, for example, this conversation between Ellis-the-character and Aimee Light, a graduate student with whom he is cheating on his wife:

> 'It's weird you said Patrick Bateman,' she said.
> 'Why?'
> 'Because I thought he looked a little like Christian Bale.'
> We were both silent for a long time, because Christian Bale was the actor who had played Patrick Bateman in the film version of *American Psycho*.
> 'But he also looked like you,' Aimee said. 'Give or take twenty years.'

For the most part, these meta-sections are the least interesting aspects of the novel — but, having said that, they are crucial to building the complex picture of a character (and an author?) haunted by his past. And although *American Psycho* is at the forefront of what 'haunts' Ellis-the-character, Patrick Bateman is only a cipher for Ellis-the-author's exploration of other ghosts that need exorcising in the book: his family tensions and regrets.

Despite the author's use of many clichéd horror tropes in this novel (the haunted house with flickering lights, the possessed doll, the dog barking at things humans can't see, the moving furniture, the mysterious phone calls, the spectres, the ghostbusters) what makes *Lunar Park* intriguing is its Gothic subtleties — the family secrets, the painfully awkward conversations, the things left unsaid, the protagonist's complicated unravelling. Ellis-the-author becomes Ellis-the-character and eventually splits into Ellis-the-character and 'the writer' (who is, possibly, Ellis-the-author overtly commenting on the fiction he's created, but equally possibly it is *not*). Over the course of the story, Ellis-the-character devolves from arrogant self-confident arse to emotionally wrecked introspective mess. Is his split personality and degeneration a sign of madness? Hallucinations resulting from years of drug abuse? 'You were simply the go-between' the writer says to Bret at one stage — which is key for interpreting the 'I' in this horror. All manifestations of Ellis are intermediaries between author and reader, author and idea, reader and idea, 'truth' and 'lies', 'fact' and 'fiction', the past that can't be ignored and the present that wants to ignore it. In other words, all versions of Ellis seem to be using literature to Figure Important Things Out.

> 'I want you to realize some things about yourself,' [says the 'murderer' on the phone to 'Bret']. 'I want you to reflect on your life. I want you to be aware of all the terrible things you have done. I want you to face the disaster that is Bret Easton Ellis.'

It's moments like this — of clarity, humanity, vulnerability — that ultimately makes the layering of so many Ellises as poignant as it is horrific.

The same can be said of Paul Haines' use of the 'I' in his short fiction. In 'Slice of Life', 'Haines' is a disgruntled office jerk who hates his boss, his job, and almost everything ... except for his *distasteful* pastime. Like Ellis, Haines-the-author splits his protagonist into separate entities: there's Haines-the-character and 'Vogon', an invisible shape-shifting alien being who adopts Haines's appearance, suggesting in more than one way that he is another manifestation of this character's already dark side.

'You're out of your warped little mind, buddy,' [says Haines-the-character to Vogon.]
  'And you're not?'
  'Point taken.'

Vogon isn't here to excuse the protagonist's aberrant behaviour, but to underline his rational-and-insane thinking. Haines-the-character seems to be as aware as the reader that Vogon isn't *real*:

Sometimes he embodies everything I fucking hate about the face I present to the world during the daylight hours. The gloating, conservative cunt knows this—he's imitated me for years now—and I wish I had the mental strength to kill him.

For a moment, we can almost ask ourselves: who is Haines talking about here? Which version is the original, which the imitation? Whatever the answer, Haines-the-character needs *mental* strength to get rid of Vogon — to oust the creature from his mind. The protagonist's struggle is internal, in this and in the other Haines-as-character stories: 'His voice echoes inside my head. "Do it."' In this case, Vogon is the whisperer, but given the circumstances it is tempting to imagine the author himself as the devil perched on Haines's shoulder.

There are similarities in characterisation between the protagonist of 'Slice of Life' and the one in 'Burning from the Inside'. All of the fictional Haineses are restless, dissatisfied with their day jobs, frequently prowling or on the move (whether walking at night, driving across bridges or travelling interstate for work) but, like Haines in 'Slice' the narrator of 'Burning' seems to be controlled by some other part of himself:

'Instead I smile—or at least something dwelling within moves my lips for me....'

Later, when speaking to a real estate agent, we see a similar thing:

'Tell the Family they've found the right tenant,' says the creature with my voice.

But is this narrator 'Paul Haines'? The afterword to 'Burning from the Inside' circumstantially locates the author within the text, but the story itself doesn't name him; the narrator uses nothing but 'I'. The afterword to this piece describes how Haines-the-author travelled to Adelaide for work as an I.T. consultant — a job Haines-the-character also has in 'The Past is a Bridge Best Left Burnt'. Author-Haines describes walking around the city of Adelaide after dark, 'watching the doors close, the streets empty, and feel any vibrancy or life left in the CBD literally boarding the buses and making their escape' — a scenario that echoes the one played out in 'Slice of Life' in which 'Haines' uses late-night walks and after-work bus rides to stalk his prey.

Likewise, the afterword for 'Father, Father' gives readers a glimpse of the 'I' that was excised from the piece — and later, in the story's republication in *The Last Days of Kali Yuga*, the 'I' that was partially reinstated. Haines tells us how this narrative — a confronting piece told from the perspective of a paedophile — originally featured characters named after Haines and his wife, a technique the author also uses in 'The Past is a Bridge Best Left Burnt'. However, he explains, the names were removed from 'Father Father':

My wife was struggling to reconcile the fictional world with our reality. I refused to bury the story, however. If I started such self-censorship now, what was the point in writing horror with regard to the monster that is man?

Two phrases in this passage immediately jump out as being crucial when approaching Haines's brilliant, chilling, and most perceptibly autobiographical work of horror, 'The Past is a Bridge Best Left Burnt': attempting to reconcile fictional worlds with reality, and writing that delves into 'the monster that is man'.

This story begins with a now-familiar fictional Haines: tired, on edge, observing the everyday through dark lenses. We also know the tale to come will be twisted, as Haines's stories generally are, but we are comfortable in the knowledge that it is fiction... And then we're confronted with this:

> I'm Paul Haines. Born thirty-six years ago in New Zealand. Now living in Melbourne, Australia, married to Jules, and have a five-month old daughter we named Isla.

This 'factual' introduction to author and protagonist irrevocably changes the way we read the rest of the story. It feels more real, more dangerous, more *raw* because it is presented as truth. Haines-the-author describes his/Haines-the-character's dissatisfaction with their lot at work. It plainly states their income and struggle with bills. It outlines their success as writers of SF. Then, dropped in casually, as unequivocal as the facts about mortgage costs and publication history, Haines tells us:

> Did I mention there is blood in my stool? No? Maybe I'm just not thinking clearly anymore. Are you?
>
> Let's test that. You think this is part of the story? That this is a story? Wrong. Not this time.

According to the Australian Bureau of Statistics, thirty percent of all suicides in the last recorded year were males aged between 30 and 34 years old.

I love my daughter more than anything else in the world.

This story is built on implications, blurred lines and the unsaid. In this short passage, we jump from fact to 'fact' to fact to a father's love for his daughter, another fact that ties all of the others together, making them as sad as they are horrifying.

I'm not going to analyse any other passages from this incredible story — I'm not going to break it by taking it apart. Like *Lunar Park*, prose and plot are strengthened by what *isn't* said, what is left to the imagination. However, compared to 'The Past is a Bridge Best Left Burnt', *Lunar Park* reads like an intellectual exercise. The insertion of 'Bret Easton Ellis' into the story seems calculated, contrived: the author seems to be featured in the book in order to achieve certain literary effects. By contrast, when Paul Haines appears in this particular story it seems unaffected. There's literary flair galore, but no cheap acrobatics, no gimmickry. This piece is nakedly honest; it confronts the horror of life without flinching. And it is impossible not to be affected by its direct and touching use of 'I':

This is not a cry for help. I'm fine.
> I just need to tell someone.
> Anyone.
> You.

---

1. Many thanks to Dr Ben Kooyman for sharing his insights on *Wes Craven's New Nightmare* and Hooper's *Midnight Movie*.

After Fight Club

Imagine the last time you were really excited to see a new film. Maybe it was the genre, maybe the cast, maybe the general plot that caught your interest — whatever it was, there was just *something* about it. And when the movie trailer started playing in theatres and on TV, you watched it that first time and thought, 'Yeah, this is for me.'

But then you realised the release date was weeks away. And all the networks kept showing that trailer — once, twice, ten times an hour. One of two things tended to happen from that point onward. Either your anticipation grew each time the commercial came on — the whole thing looked more and more awesome — or, in seeing the same parts repeatedly, you started to suspect that that was pretty much it, the whole shebang. All the good bits had been crammed into that thirty-second snippet, it seemed, and so your interest in the movie waned.

The latter is, unfortunately, how I feel now about most of Chuck Palahniuk's novels. I read *Fight Club* over a decade ago, and was utterly wowed by it; but having just devoured it again along with several of Palahniuk's subsequent books in quick succession — *Survivor*, *Invisible Monsters*, *Choke*, *Lullaby*, *Diary* and *Haunted* — I can't help but feel like I've just watched a trailer for *Fight Club: Redux*, over and over and over again.

Addressing The Reader

These novels — with the exception, perhaps, of *Haunted* — are consistently written in the second person, some more overtly than others. The narrator of *Fight Club* invites readers into Tyler Durden's nihilistic world by addressing them directly, though usually unobtrusively. 'Would you just look at his sculpted hair,' he says, describing Big Bob. 'You wake up at SeaTac... You wake up at LAX,' he says in Chapter 3. 'You see a guy come to fight club for the first time, and his ass is a loaf of white bread,' he says, when things are just getting started. And much later, 'The rule in Project Mayhem is you have to trust Tyler.' Readers are drawn in by this unreliable narrative voice; we're included in fight club, in the support groups, in Project Mayhem, but we nevertheless remain at a distance.

In later books, Palahniuk refuses us the comfort of being bystanders: the opening passages seem to directly address the reader, even when it's clear that the 'you' refers to another character in the novel. 'By the time you read this,' the second page of *Diary* begins, 'you'll be older than you remember.' We know the diarist is writing to Peter Wilmot, who is hospitalised and in a coma, but we cannot help but see ourselves in this statement. As if to reinforce this feeling, the narrator goes on to say, 'Let's look in the mirror. Really look at your face. Look at your eyes, your mouth. This is what you think you know best.' This is a trick Palahniuk uses consistently in his books, increasingly so after *Fight Club*. He turns the lens onto the viewers, so to speak. Implicates readers in the horrible realities about which they're reading. He tells them what they should think. 'If you're going to read this, don't bother,' says the narrator of *Choke*. 'After a couple of pages, you won't want to be here. So forget it. Go away. Get out while you're still in one piece. Save yourself. ...What happens here is first going to piss you off. After that it just gets worse and worse.'

In its very first line, *Invisible Monsters* also tells us we're in the wrong place: 'Where you're supposed to be is some big West Hills wedding reception in a big manor house...' whereas *Survivor* calls out in the beginning, asking us to stick around: 'Maybe this thing is working. I don't know. If you can even hear me, I don't know. But if you can hear me, listen.' Meanwhile, *Lullaby* tries to push us away again by explaining how the tale we're about to read is told from at least one remove: 'The problem with every story is you tell it after the fact.'

Alas, another problem, after the fact, is seeing how every one of these stories is so very similar. So repetitive.

The Chorus

The most repeated lines from Palahniuk's debut novel are undoubtedly, 'The first rule about fight club is you don't talk about fight club. The second rule about fight club ... is you don't talk about fight club.' But in terms of memorable, now-classic *Fight Club* lines, a close second would have to be those spoken by 'Joe's' body parts. After reading an old magazine article in which pieces of the human body speak — 'I am Jane's Uterus. I am Joe's Prostate.' — the narrator frequently uses 'Joe's' guts as voice-boxes for his emotions:

> Hearing this, I am totally Joe's Gallbladder... I am Joe's Raging Bile Duct... I am Joe's Grinding Teeth... I am Joe's

Inflamed Flaring Nostrils... I am Joe's White Knuckles... I am Joe's Enraged, Inflamed Sense of Rejection.

This was *such* a cool technique in *Fight Club* — so new, so inventive, so fresh. But just as jokes become less and less funny the more frequently they're told, this sort of repetition — what Palahniuk refers to as a 'chorus' — becomes less impressive in subsequent novels. In *Diary*, Misty Marie Kleinman's mental state is reflected in recurring weather reports, which begin on the first page.

> 'The weather today is increasing concern followed by full-blown dread.'
>
> 'The weather today is an increasing trend toward denial.'
>
> 'The weather today is partly angry, leading to resignation and ultimatums.'
>
> 'Just for the record, the weather today is partly suspicious with chances of betrayal.'
>
> 'Just for the record, the weather today is increasing turmoil with a possible physical and emotional breakdown.'

Just for the record, 'just for the record' is another of Palahniuk's overused choruses, which also appears in *Survivor*. In *Invisible Monsters*, the narrator was once a model; her chorus comes in the form of a photographer insider her head, giving instructions, telling her how to feel:

> Give me lust, baby.
> > Flash.
> > Give me malice.
> > Flash.
> > Give me detached existential ennui.
> > Flash...
> > Give me homesickness.

Flash.

Give me nostalgic childhood yearnings.

And so on. There are too many to discuss in this column — some books, like *Diary*, have several choruses; others, like *Choke*, have whole chapters that act like refrains. When these phrases are added to texts that are already so alike — in characterisation, in their tendency to use specific medical jargon when describing characters, in their encyclopaedic descriptions of pharmaceuticals and STDs — the effect is increasingly contrived, increasingly dull.

Of course, that's probably the point.

Reducing stories to single, repetitive lines might serve the same purpose as using the second person perspective, for instance, or breaking people down to their anatomical parts: it makes everyone a generic 'you'. It dehumanises. Universalises. It lulls readers into a false sense of familiarity before the narrative can shock them back out of it.

'Better' Than Real Life

Each of the books discussed here features people with similar quirks: there are tortured artists (*Diary*, *Haunted*), attention-seekers (*Choke*, *Fight Club*, *Invisible Monsters*, *Survivor*), experts in the many and varied uses of narcotics (*Choke*, *Invisible Monsters*, *Lullaby* — well, all of them, really). There are therapy junkies, sex addicts, fraudsters, trailer trash, delusionals, sacrificial women, scammers and liars and doctors-who-aren't-really and grown-ups who haven't quite grown up. And many of these characters seem to exist in order to play God. To shake things up. To control — or disrupt, or end — other people's boring lives.

'People had been working for so many years to make the world a safe, organized place,' says Victor, the narrator in *Choke*:

> Nobody realized how boring it would become. With the whole world property-lined and speed-limited and zoned and taxed and regulated, with everyone tested and registered and addressed and recorded. Nobody had left much room for adventure, except maybe the kind you could buy. On a roller coaster. At a movie. Still, it would always be that kind of faux excitement. You know the dinosaurs aren't going to eat the kids. The test audiences have outvoted any chance of even a major faux disaster. And because there's no possibility of real disaster, real risk, we're left with no chance for real salvation. Real elation. Real excitement. Joy. Discovery. Invention.
>
> The laws that keep us safe, these same laws condemn us to boredom.

This is also allegedly why Victor pretends to choke on his food every night while dining out: 'To showcase just one brave stranger. To save just one more person from boredom. It's not *just* for the money. It's not *just* for the adoration.'

In *Lullaby*, Carl Streator and Helen Hoover Boyle have discovered a magical 'culling spell' — an eight-line children's poem that, when read in full, instantly kills the listener. For much of the narrative, they drive around the United States trying to collect all copies of the deadly book of *Poems from Around the World* — ostensibly to save people from accidentally committing murder. But it soon becomes clear that the pair isn't acting for the good of society, but to maintain control over it:

> 'This isn't about love and hate,' Helen says.

> It's about control. People don't sit and read a poem to kill their child. They just want the child to sleep. They just want to dominate. No matter how much you love someone, you still want to have your own way.

That's essentially what Project Mayhem is all about. As in *Fight Club* (and *Haunted*, *Choke*, *Diary*, *Survivor*, and *Invisible Monsters*) the characters in *Lullaby* want to be in control of shaking people from the stupor of happy boredom: 'the plan is to undermine the illusion of safety and comfort in people's lives.'

In *Haunted*, a group of eccentric characters go off on what is supposed to be a three-month writing retreat — each person's backstory is told, *Canterbury Tales*-style, in a series of interconnected short poems and stories penned by the characters themselves. Like many of Palahniuk's creatures, this bunch is self-consciously aware that they're unconventional and, as a result, somehow more awake than the rest of the 'normal' population. As they're travelling on the bus, taking a road trip (as so many of the 'outsiders' in these novels do) to their secret destination, they remark:

> The dreaming world, they'd think we were crazy. Those people still in bed, they'd be asleep another hour, then washing their faces, under their arms, and between their legs, before going to the same work they did every day. Living that same life, every day.

In other words, normal (boring) people are sleeping through their (boring) lives. The need for the everyman to wake up is one of the most common themes in Palahniuk's work, which has its roots in *Fight Club*, Chapter 3: 'You wake up at Air Harbor International… You wake up at O'Hare. You wake up at LaGuardia. You wake up at Logan… You wake up at Dulles... You wake up at Love Field....' and so on. It is no coincidence that this chapter, with these repeated wake-ups, is the one in which the narrator meets Tyler Durden — the man responsible for 'waking' him from his IKEA-filled, suit-and-tie-wearing existence. The man who causes the narrator's insomnia. The man behind Project Mayhem. In *Haunted*, the writers are up and on the bus by 4.30am, which makes them feel like adventurers, explorers, astronauts. They are proud to be 'Awake while [everyone else] slept.'

No matter their gender or their settings, so many of Palahniuk's characters are caught up with teaching the faceless, generic mass of humanity a lesson by example: 'To create a race of masters from a race of slaves, Mr Whittier said, to teach a controlled group of people how to create their own lives....' Note the pun in the writing teacher's name here: he is 'wittier' than everyone else, because he is doing something to upset the status quo. He is rescuing the other characters, whether they like it or not. In other words, he has a saviour complex — just like everyone else.

Tyler Durden appears in *Fight Club* to save people from being mindless drones like the ones described in the novel's first chapter: 'You do the little job you're trained to do. Pull a lever. Push a button. You don't understand any of it, and then you just die.' There's no point to anything. Everything is a repetition of what's come before. Everyone is asleep. Everyone is a space monkey. But being part of Project Mayhem, breaking out, rebelling, even at the risk of death — well, 'This was better than real life.'

What happens afterwards may not be the average Joe's idea of salvation, but from the characters' perspectives, their drastic, often drug-fuelled actions are precisely that. 'I don't expect you to understand,' says the narrator of *Survivor*, after explaining how random strangers phone him at all hours on the verge of suicide, and he encourages them to kill themselves. 'Try barbiturates and alcohol with your head inside a dry cleaning bag,' he says. 'Pull the trigger or don't. I'm with her right now. She's not going to die alone, but I don't have all night.' Palahniuk's solutions to middle-class ennui are typically satirical, increasingly over-the-top. In order to save people, the narrator of *Survivor* tells them to die. Carl and Helen kill dozens of people in *Lullaby* in order to 'save the children'. In an attempt to preserve the lifestyle of Waytansea Island (another pun), Misty's mother-in-law and the town doctor keep her trapped in a hotel for weeks; just like Mr Whittier keeps his writing students trapped in a surreal hotel for three months during their 'retreat' in *Haunted*; just as Victor and his mother are trapped in the past in *Choke*, while others are trapped in the hospital. All of it is done for good reason, they seem to think. It's done for the good of others.

At the same time, characters go to extremes in order to force other people to save them. The narrator of *Survivor* hijacks an airplane. In *Invisible Monsters*, the protagonist goes to drastic lengths to stop being beautiful and boring: 'What I need to do is fuck up so bad I can't save myself.' Meanwhile her companion, a drag queen named Brandy Alexander, plans to undergo sex reassignment surgery — not because she really wants to become a woman, but because 'it's just the biggest mistake [she] can think to make. It's stupid and destructive…. That's why [she has] to go through with it.' In *Lullaby*, Carl wants to get caught by the police; he wants to turn himself in, just to leave his fate up to the authorities. Similarly, Victor's mother in *Choke* breaks law after law in order to 'save' her son. Breaking the law and destabilising social norms seem to be the only ways these characters can be saved from their own fakery, from the otherwise inescapable humdrum of the everyday, from life.

In *Choke*, Victor fakes choking to death in order, he says, to give others the chance to feel like saviours. But in so doing, Victor is selfishly seeking an escape from the problems in his life. Instead of taking a road trip, as the characters do in *Invisible Monsters* and *Lullaby* for example, Victor escapes into the warm embraces of strangers — either through casual sex, or from being 'saved' by them in restaurants. Gasping for breath, Victor cries, night after night, while snuggling into his 'rescuer's' embrace. He revels in the feelings of calm and release that come with this post-salvation cuddle — much like the narrator in *Fight Club* cries for release while burying himself in Big Bob's immense hug at the Remaining Men Together therapy sessions. It's the same escape — for characters, and for readers — over and over and over.

In these novels, Palahniuk has come up with a template for his stories that has earned him a cult following. Minimalist writing. Screwed-up characters. Nihilism. Repetitive choruses. Wittiness. Surreal, humorous satire. The issue I've got with these books is certainly not the content, nor the subject matter. It's not the *what* of them that's grown tiresome. It's the *how*. How much they repeat themselves. How similar they are in technique. How they are inherently about waking up, but insist on presenting these shake-ups in now-conventional ways. How much they echo *Fight Club* — and like all echoes, they aren't as crisp as the original note. And after reading these novels back-to-back-to-back, this passage from *Fight Club* rings truer than ever:

> 'Go home, tonight, and forget about fight club. I think fight club has served its purpose, don't you?'

Wide Open Fear

AUSTRALIAN HORROR AND GOTHIC FICTION
(C. 2004-2014)

In her introduction to *Australis Imaginarium* (2010), Tehani Wessely succinctly summarises an idea that has become something of a truism when it comes to discussing horror and dark fantasy stories with Australian settings:

> There's simply something about the vastness of this land and the many weird, wild and dangerous creatures that populate it that lends itself to terrifying tales.

Looking at Australian short fiction published in recent years, we can see exactly what Wessely means. These stories are riddled with manifestations of 'Australian Gothic'. Many of them depict rural isolation: people alone in the desert, in the bush, by the sea. Underlining human and supernatural threats is nature itself, harsh and unforgiving; over it all hangs an endless, suffocating sky. The settings in these narratives are more than just unsettling or uncanny; there's an *unheimlich* quality to this country's wilderness, which makes it clear that most characters — human or otherwise — are unwelcome. *Leave*, they seem to say. *You don't belong here.*

When we think of Gothic literature — Australian or otherwise — several themes or features immediately come to mind: ghosts from the past (literal and metaphorical) rising up to oppress the stories' protagonists; a sense of discomfort, of being unwholesome, resulting from breaking social taboos; overwhelming darkness, hopelessness, claustrophobia, and disintegration. Australia's colonial/convict history is an obvious source of inspiration for this type of horror — but there are so many Australian Gothic stories set in the colonial period that we'll have to save discussing them for another time. Instead, I want to focus on stories that feature 'the vastness of this land' — either as a backdrop to dark short stories, or as a fundamental part of the horror itself.

In Sue Isle's 'The Painted Girl' (*Nightsiders*), we get the impression that nature is obliterating the past as well as shaping the present. Bushfires rage in this story's opening, ravaging the landscape and making it indistinguishable from Australia as we currently know it. At the same time, fire is a controlling force: it shepherds the characters, driving them inward, making them run. Bushfires function in a similar way in my story 'White and Red in the Black' (*Dead Red Heart*); burning earth fences the characters in, keeping them contained, terrified within the confines of their homestead. In Paul Haines' 'The Past is a Bridge Best Left Burnt' (*The Last Days of Kali Yuga*), we don't see the fire itself, but its smoke. Like a bell jar descending on the city, a grey pall echoes the protagonist's increasingly dark thoughts, enhancing the sense that he's being stifled, suffocating in his life.

Drought, like fire, often turns the land to dust in these Australian stories, obliterating the past and making the future look bleak. After offering glimpses of scorched, otherworldly trees and black earth, the final lines of Sean

William's poem 'Parched' (*Sprawl*) are a haunting refrain, and a promise of worse to come: 'it never rains / for long / here.' And in 'Virgin Jackson' (*Australis Imaginarium*) Marianne de Pierres takes us to an inhospitable, not-so-distant time in the future, where hot north-east winds 'evaporated the fluid from your body in seconds' and 'scoured the *wayback* into grotesque landforms, sharp gullies and dust ball plains.' Images of dusty, desert (and deserted) plains feature most prominently in these short stories: often cast in shades of sunset, representations of the country's red heart seem to be used as shorthand for the wide open fear of the Australian landscape.

The dangers inherent in the desert are usually referred to within the first few pages — and often in the first paragraph — of these tales. Not just to set the scene; these descriptions instantly add a horrific tone to each piece, to suggest that things can only get worse in what's to follow. For example, Jason Fischer opens 'Undead Camels Ate Their Flesh' (*Dreaming Again*) like so:

> With its usual efficiency, the sun blazed down on bugger-all. It was the Outback, with nothing for hundreds of miles but heat, dust and flies.

This offers a bleak, uncompromising picture of Australia, much like the first lines of Joanna Fay's 'Black Heart' (*Dead Red Heart*):

> It was time to die. That was why she'd come here, to the red land. The sky swept over here, horizon to horizon, uncompromising scarlet. The colour of her unlife, like the sands stretched wide to meet it.

Likewise, Dirk Strasser's 'The Dark Under the Sun'

(*Australis Imaginarium*) captures the feeling that this is not a place where life thrives:

> There was red flatness as far as he could see, like a fire that had been trampled to death by a thousand feet, but which had somehow managed to keep its heat while its flames had been killed. Out of the heat grew clumps of grass and twisted, black-bodied trees, but they were so few and far between that it was as if rather than being in the process of living, they were in the process of dying.

Even when the stories take place after dark, the sun, the desert and its denizens are treated as pervasive, immediate concerns. Though sunset brings with it cooler temperatures, in 'Sun Falls' (*Dead Red Heart*) Angela Slatter reminds us of 'the sounds of the night: cicadas, possums, snakes, lizards, hares, wallabies. All manner of nasties that don't come out in the sunlight.' While Slatter's story cuts with black humour, Alan Baxter's 'Punishment of the Sun' (*Dead Red Heart*) adds a more melancholy edge to the land after sunset. Baxter describes a 'world beyond stygian and dead' with 'dry, dusty paddocks with dry, dusty horses, ribs like xylophone keys through thin, scabby hides. The orange desolation dragged on as far as hope would last in every direction. Too young to leave this desiccated hole, [Annie] grudgingly endured.' This notion of Australia as a 'Hell' or a 'hole' to be endured is also present in the opening paragraph of Pete Kempshall's 'Signature Walk' (*Sprawl*), in which a little girl asks:

> 'Where's Australia, Granddad?' … He held her gaze and pointed straight down at the ground. She shook her head. 'No, Granddad, you're wrong … Australia can't be down there,' said the girl with absolute assurance. 'That's where Hell is.'

Marty Young also draws on hellish imagery to set the 'horror' tone of his story, 'Desert Blood' (*Dead Red Heart*):

> The world began to bleed as the sun melted into the horizon. Hell was leaking, its blood seeping up from the sand and the sunset itself to reflect in the slow-moving Cooper Creek next to them.

The sun setting over expanses of red sand lends itself to plenty of lovely Gothic imagery: crumbling buildings in silhouette, darkness limned with blood and crimson wastelands. However, the Australian sky is perhaps at its most frightening, its most suffocating, during daylight hours. 'The sky was blue as a vein the day I killed my father,' begins Stephen M Irwin's 'Hive' (*Macabre*), but it 'wouldn't stay that way; the strange, ice-fire blue eventually gave way to eerie grey, then to the red of sick blood.' The sky's disintegration from brightness to blood foreshadows the young protagonist's psychological turmoil, his vivid dreams and descent into a sort of temporary madness. Moreover, it reflects Michael's very personal horror. By contrast, the sky in Sean Williams' 'Passing the Bone' (*Australis Imaginarium*) is 'a blue sheet pressing down on the world' that seems designed to stifle everyone, like a pillow pressed over the face. The vastness of the Australian wilderness is contained only by leaves and sky in Margo Lanagan's 'Pig's Whisper' (*Agog! Ripping Reads*)

> The bush was vast around them, immense above them; its frail roof of leaves was a sky within a sky.

Out here, the children are frightfully exposed; they are plunged into Australian lore, and must figure their own way out.

Two stories published in recent years are standouts, in my opinion, for integrating characters and their plights from the world in which they exist. The first is 'Smoking, Waiting for the Dawn' (*Dreaming Again*) by Jason Nahrung. This piece marks its territory by describing dusty red land, but where many of the examples I've given above use Australia's unforgiving climate and its deserts as a backdrop to the action, this piece's setting is integral in conveying the weariness, exhaustion, and wonderful bleakness that are driving forces in the plot:

> George stood by the bleached skeleton of the Wyandra stockyards, breathing in dust and sun-baked silence. The rust-red roofs of the township shimmered in the heat haze, and from what he could see, his old stomping ground hadn't fared much better than he had in the past twenty years: tired, forlorn, running out of time.

This is Australian Gothic. Hopelessness and the certainty of defeat right from the word go. A relentless sense of doom ingrained in the very dirt. And the characters forging on, regardless. A similar effect is achieved in Nahrung's 'Wraiths' (*Winds of Change*); there is a feeling of not-quite-acceptance, a stoic weariness in the face of 'natural' threats, established right from the first paragraph:

> The dust wraiths struck with all the speed and surprise and finality of a slamming door. We should've felt it coming, but we didn't. Maybe it was the heat, dulling our senses with its touch of lazy. Maybe it was just our time and, on some level, down deep, we knew it and ignored the signs. Or maybe they'd just got tired of us and decided to end it, once and for all.

Heat, dust, sun and desert are embodied in Nahrung's characterisations; these people are the landscape, and its chilling horrors, personified — you can practically hear red dust grinding between their teeth, in their bones — which makes this authors' stories essential reading for anyone interested in Australian horror.

The second piece that shouldn't be missed is Paul Haines' 'Burning from the Inside' (*The Last Days of Kali Yuga*). Although this story is mostly set in Adelaide — it integrates city settings with the more iconic 'sunburnt country' imagery — it captures the spirit of Australian horror in an absolutely chilling way. In Haines' fiction, setting is never a trope or a cheap add-on. And in this piece in particular, it's impossible to separate the protagonist from his surroundings. From the first line, we're given insight into his mindset, and how Adelaide has helped to shape it:

> I'd like to say I feel unsettled here, but I don't.

Right away, we learn that this setting is something we should be afraid of, something we should feel unsettled by. At the same time, this line immediately hooks us into the true point of the story: this city, this setting, can be unforgiving and scary, but it is the protagonist's perception of Adelaide — and his being so at home in this place — that makes us shudder to the core.

> From my hotel room I can see the river Torrens snaking through the park, the lush of leaf in contrast to the desert sands that lap at the shoreline this city makes. The sun is settling on the horizon, finally a thing of beauty rather than the raging father in the sky, now its urgency is almost spent. One can imagine the river, that gurgle of water, a searing temptation for the heat bursting forth from the dead heart of

this red island continent. A thirst to be quenched? Or something to be destroyed, the last bastion of hope holding back the inevitable conquest that shapes this dry land? Ornate spires reach for the heavens, dozens of them, over trees, nestled between crossroads and office buildings, the cross of Christ thrust up bold and true. One only has to glance in any direction to find the house of God here. From this spot alone I spy the Holy Trinity, Scots, St Patrick's, St Peter's, Christ's, Brougham Place and Immanuel. And here I am. In the City of Churches. Adelaide. My new home for the foreseeable future. The murder capital of Australia.

There are so many contrasts, so much tension in this paragraph alone: city/country, drought/drowning, heaven/hell, life/death, past/present; it is a complex and disturbing sketch of the city, and the land surrounding it. In this story, more than any other, the setting — with its deadly creatures, ruthless atmosphere and horrific history — *possesses* the main character. It haunts and inhabits him. It tears him apart even as it gives him purpose. It will not leave him alone.

This is Australian horror. And it is absolutely terrifying.

About the Author

Lisa L. Hannett has had over 75 short stories appear in venues including *Clarkesworld*, *Weird Tales*, *Apex*, *The Dark* and in Year's Best anthologies in Australia, Canada and the US. She has won the Ditmar for Best Novel, an Australian Shadows Award, and four Aurealis Awards, including Best Collection for her first book, *Bluegrass Symphony*, which was also nominated for a World Fantasy Award. Her newest collection of short stories is *Songs for Dark Seasons* (2020). You can find her online at www.lisahannett.com.

instagram.com/LisaLHannett

Also by Lisa L. Hannett

Bluegrass Symphony
Lament for the Afterlife
Songs for Dark Seasons

With Angela Slatter

Midnight and Moonshine
The Female Factory

Thank You For Buying This Brain Jar Press Chapbook

To receive special offers, bonus content, and info on new releases and other great reads, visit us online at www.BrainJarPress.com

www.ingramcontent.com/pod-product-compliance
Lightning Source LLC
Chambersburg PA
CBHW021453080526
44588CB00009B/829